DATE DUE

SEA LIONS

Jen Green

Grolier
an imprint of
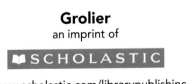
SCHOLASTIC
www.scholastic.com/librarypublishing

Published 2008 by Grolier
An imprint of Scholastic Library Publishing
Old Sherman Turnpike, Danbury,
Connecticut 06816

For The Brown Reference Group plc
Project Editor: Jolyon Goddard
Copy-editors: Ann Baggaley, Lisa Hughes
Picture Researcher: Clare Newman
Designers: Jeni Child, Lynne Ross,
        Sarah Williams
Managing Editor: Bridget Giles

Volume ISBN-13: 978-0-7172-6285-4
Volume ISBN-10: 0-7172-6285-5

**Library of Congress
Cataloging-in-Publication Data**

Nature's children. Set 3.
    p. cm.
Includes bibliographical references and
index.
ISBN 13: 978-0-7172-8082-7
ISBN 10: 0-7172-8082-9
1. Animals--Encyclopedias, Juvenile. I.
Grolier Educational (Firm)
QL49.N384 2008
590.3--dc22
                    2007031568

Printed and bound in China

PICTURE CREDITS

Front Cover: **Nature PL**: Pete Oxford.

Back Cover: **Alamy**: Richard Dirscherl,
Sunny Photography; **Shutterstock**: Andrea
Haase, Wrangler.

Alamy: Rob Francis 17; **FLPA**: Tui De
Roy/Minden Pictures 21, 37, Suzi
Eszterhaus/Minden Pictures 41, Malcolm
Schyl 22; **Nature PL**: Mark Carwardine 34,
Brandon Cole 6, Suzi Eszterhaus 2–3, 29,
Pete Oxford 4, 26–27, 38, 46, Doug Perrine
10, Gabriel Rojo 5, 45; **Photolibrary.com**:
Shane Moore 9; **Shutterstock**: Andrea
Haase 18, Richard Harvey 33, Nik Niklz 30,
Wrangler 13; **Still Pictures**: Fotototo 14,
Kevin Schafer 42.

Contents

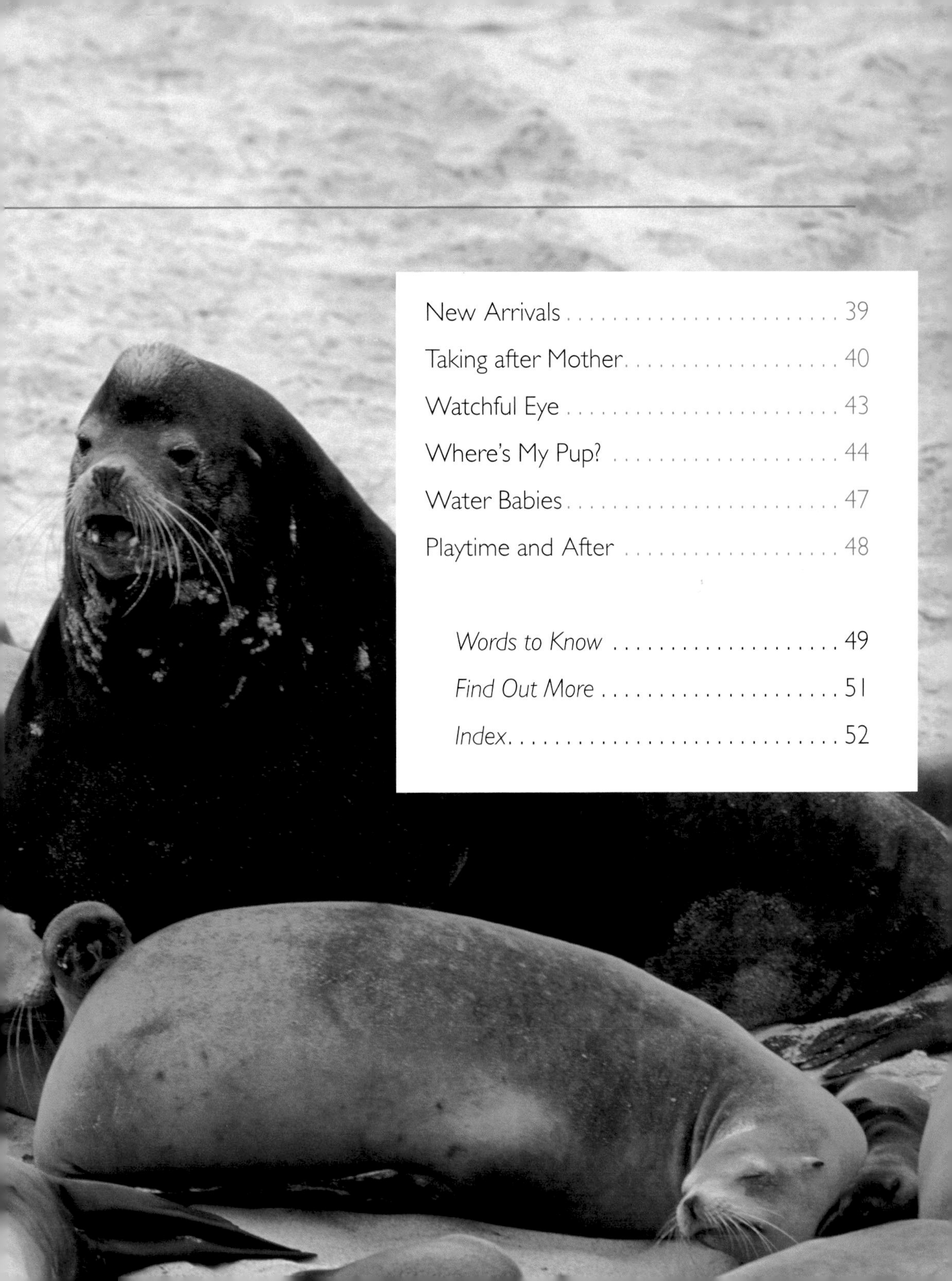

FACT FILE: Sea Lions

Class	Mammals (Mammalia)
Order	Seal family (Pinnipedia)
Family	Eared seals (Otariidae)
Genera	Five genera
Species	Six species, including the northern, or Steller, sea lion (*Eumetopias jubata*) and the California sea lion (*Zalophus californianus*)
World distribution	Depends on the species
Habitat	Coastal waters and on shore
Distinctive physical characteristics	Torpedo-shaped body and doglike head with small ears; strong front flippers for swimming; rear flippers can be turned forward for walking on land
Habits	Live in herds; playful in the water; males fight to control groups of females
Diet	Fish, shellfish, squid, octopus, and seabirds

Introduction

Which animal barks like a dog and swims like a fish? Which animal is clumsy on land, yet fast and graceful in the water? It's a sea lion, of course. Sea lions often perform tricks in an aquarium. These tame animals are smart, agile, and easy to train. In the wild sea lions are also swift hunters that prefer being in the company of others. The females make caring mothers, whereas the males can be big bullies!

Young South American sea lions like to hang out together.

A roaring northern sea lion shows its sharp lower teeth.

Seal Family

Sea lions are members of the seal family. Scientists call this family the **pinnipeds**, which means "fin-footed." True to this name, a seal's **webbed feet** work rather like a fish's fins. They push against the water, propelling the seal forward.

There are 34 **species**, or types, of seals in the seal family. The family is divided into three groups. Sea lions and their close relatives, fur seals, make up one group called eared seals. The other big group is the true, or earless, seals. In fact, all seals have ears, but "earless" seals have no earflaps covering their ears. In contrast, a sea lion's earflaps are easily visible. The third group of seals contains just one species, the walrus, which lives in the Arctic.

Watery World

The best place to see sea lions is not in an aquarium, but swimming in the wild! All members of the seal family are **aquatic mammals**. These animals are completely at home in water. A few types of seals live in lakes, but sea lions prefer the saltwater of the oceans. Sea lions spend most of their time in the shallow waters close to shore.

There are several types of sea lions, living in different parts of the oceans, including off South America, Australia, and New Zealand. Two species of sea lions swim off the shores of western North America. Northern sea lions live in the cold waters of the North Pacific. Those are also called Steller sea lions. California sea lions swim in warmer waters, from around Vancouver Island in Canada, south to the long slender **peninsula** of Baja California, in Mexico.

A herd of northern sea lions gathers on a beach.

A sea lion twists and turns acrobatically underwater.

Super Swimmers

Few creatures are as quick and as graceful in water as sea lions. Sea lions spin, weave, and somersault like underwater acrobats. The sea lion's sleek, torpedo-shaped body slips easily through water. The animal swims along by flapping its slender front flippers up and down, much like how a bird flaps its wings.

With a few lazy flaps of its flippers, a sea lion cruises along at about 15 miles (24 km) per hour. A California sea lion in a hurry can achieve a top speed of 25 miles (40 km) per hour, making it the speed champion of the seal family.

Deep Down

In addition to being excellent swimmers, sea lions are also amazing divers. California sea lions usually dive to depths of about 80 feet (25 m). But they can go as deep as 500 feet (150 m) if they choose. When a seal dives, special flaps close its ears and nostrils, so water doesn't get in.

Sea lions usually stay underwater for three to five minutes. However, unlike fish, which breathe underwater using their **gills**, seal lions have to return to the water's surface to breathe air. A sea lion's nostrils are located on the top of its snout. That position allows the sea lion to inhale air with minimum effort—just by moving its head slightly above the water's surface—when hunting underwater.

All sea mammals, including sea lions, seals, walruses, whales, and dolphins, have to surface to breathe air.

13

An Australian sea lion
struts along a beach.

Landlubbers

In the water, the sea lion's webbed hind flippers are mainly used for steering and maneuvering. The hind feet are most useful, however, when the sea lion heaves itself out of the water onto the land.

Sea lions can tuck their hind legs under their body. Using all four limbs, they are able to bounce along the shore at quite a speed. They are a lot quicker and more agile on land than their relatives, the earless seals. These seals cannot gather their back legs under them, so they can only crawl along on their belly, like a giant caterpillar.

Sea lions use their ability to move quickly on land to slip into the water if danger threatens. They also like to dive off rocks at the water's edge. These clever animals watch the waves carefully before jumping. They wait until there is no danger of a giant breaker sweeping them up and hurling them against the rocks.

A Waterproof Coat

Sea lions stay warm in cold water with the help of a thick fur coat. Their hair is so fine and dense that water never reaches their skin. Bubbles of air trapped in the fur help to prevent the animal's body heat from escaping. Sea lions are able to stay in the water for hours and hours without ever feeling cold.

As a sea lion swims, plays, and scrambles about on the shore, its coat wears thin. A tattered coat is not very effective at keeping body heat in. So once a year, the animal sheds its old fur in patches, and grows a new coat. This process, called **molting**, happens each spring. At this time the sea lion spends a lot of time out of the cold water, so a ragged coat doesn't matter so much. The new fur soon grows in, which again enables the sea lion to stay warm in frigid waters.

This sea lion is molting its ragged old coat and growing a thick new one.

A sea lion rests
in the sun.

Warm and Cool

In addition to fur, sea lions have a layer of fat just under their skin. This layer, called **blubber**, keeps body heat in and cold out. With the help of their blubber, northern sea lions can swim quite happily in freezing waters among chunks of floating ice! Other water-loving animals, such as whales, polar bears, and penguins, have blubber, too.

In fact, rather than feeling the cold, sea lions suffer from the opposite problem—they can overheat on land in summer. To cool off, they pant like dogs or wave their flippers in the air. The flippers don't have blubber, so they act like mini radiators, giving off body heat. If the sea lion is still too hot, it will take a cooling dip in the ocean.

A Fishy Diet

Like all seals, sea lions are **predators**. They get all their food from the ocean. Herring, cod, sardines, and greenling are among their favorite fish. They also hunt squids and octopuses, and sometimes seabirds such as guillemots.

The sea lion chases after a twisting fish, before grasping its **prey** in its jaws. Sea lions don't do much chewing. If the prey is too big to be swallowed whole, the hunter shakes it violently to break it into bite-size chunks, which it then eats.

Sea lions mostly hunt at night, either alone or in the company of others. If a school of herring swims by, sea lions napping on the shore dash into the water to join the feast.

Striped snappers dart swiftly away as sea lions approach.

By pushing itself up on its front flippers, a sea lion gets a better view of its surroundings.

Seeing Underwater

Human eyes aren't suited to seeing underwater. But sea lions can see well even in the dark depths of the ocean. In deep water, the pupils in the center of their eyes help them see by opening wide to let in as much light as possible. Their eyes also have a clear, protective layer that helps them to focus underwater.

On land, the sea lion's eyelids protect its eyes, just as a person's eyelids do. Out of water, their eyes tend to water freely. Sea lions often look as if they are crying! In fact, the tears carry away grit and sand that might harm their eyes. That helps the animal stay bright-eyed and healthy.

Feeling the Way

Sea lions have sensitive whiskers on their snout. They use them to feel their way through the murky ocean. When sea lions hunt at night, their whiskers are even more important.

A sea lion's whiskers are attached to nerves that send signals to its brain. These "feelers" are so delicate the animal can tell the difference between a strand of slippery seaweed and an octopus's tentacles. Sea lions living in aquariums use their whiskers to help balance objects, such as a ball on the end of their nose.

Hearing and Smell

As well as sharp eyes and sensitive whiskers, sea lions also have good hearing and a keen sense of smell. A female sea lion can tell her baby, or **pup**, from all the others on the beach just by its smell. But because a sea lion's nostrils close when it dives underwater, its sense of smell is useful only on land.

Luckily, the sea lion can hear both in and out of the water. A sea lion often barks underwater to let other sea lions know it is there. On land the animal twists its small earflaps around to pinpoint the exact source of a sound, in the same way that a pet dog cocks its ears.

A group of California sea lions lives around the Galápagos Islands, off the coast of South America.

Big Heads

California sea lions have brown fur. The females and young are buff, or light tan, in color. The adult males, called **bulls**, are a rich chocolate brown. But when the fur of both male and female sea lions gets wet, it looks almost black.

Male California sea lions grow to about 8 feet (2.5 m) long and weigh about 600 pounds (300 kg). The females, or **cows**, are much smaller, and weigh only about 200 pounds (100 kg). An adult bull grows a bony crest on the top of his head. It looks similar to a peaked cap. This crest gives the animal its scientific name, *Zalophus californianus*. The name means "big head from California."

A bull California sea lion, with a large crest on his head, watches over cows and pups.

A sea lion roars at
a passing ship.

Noisy Northerners

Northern sea lions are larger than their Californian cousins. The bulls grow to 11 feet (3.3 m) long and weigh up to 2,500 pounds (1,100 kg). That's about the same weight as a small car or a polar bear. In general, animals are bigger in colder regions. A big bulky body shape keeps in body heat more effectively than a slimmer body shape. The male sea lion's huge blubbery bulk keeps him warm in the icy water. As with California sea lions, the cow is only about one-third of the bull's size.

Sea lions don't look at all like the lions of Africa. But when the northern sea lion roars it sounds exactly like a real lion. That is why sea lions have "lion" in their name.

Salty Sea Dogs

Sea lions are sociable animals. They like the company of others, both in and out of the water. Groups of sea lions can be especially noisy on land. They make loud honking or "uhh uhh" grunting noises. They also growl and bark like dogs, which is why sailors of long ago used to call them sea dogs.

Female sea lions bark to locate their pup. The males bark to warn away rival males and also to warn the whole group of danger. Sea lions can be very nervous creatures. The sight of a human can disturb them and make them bark loudly. The whole group will then start to gallop down to the water.

A group of sea lions dozes on a beach.

An orca hunts a sea lion pup on the edge of the shore.

34

Menace in the Sea

Sea lions need only fear a few creatures. Their two great enemies are the top hunters in the oceans—sharks and orcas, or killer whales.

The sea lion's only defense against these huge, sharp-toothed hunters is its speed and agility. A sea lion must twist and turn to avoid its predators' snapping jaws. The safest action is often to race ashore. But even there the sea lion has to be careful. Orcas sometimes slide onto the sand to snatch an unwary sea lion. Both sharks and orcas target young or sickly sea lions. Mothers must be very careful to always watch out for their pups.

Breeding Time

In late spring to early summer, sea lions come ashore to breed. Northern sea lions like to breed on rocky beaches. California sea lions choose sandy or rocky beaches backed by cliffs. The stretch of coast where seals breed is called a **rookery**.

Bull California sea lions come ashore first. Each tries to set up his own little **territory**. The males squabble over the best spots on the beach. A lot of roaring, growling, and barking goes on, as each male tries to frighten away the others. Sometimes two big bulls square up and try to bite each other. But most of the squabbles end without serious injury.

When the males have divided the beach into territories, the cows come ashore. Each male wants as many cows as possible in his **harem**, or group. A big male may gather as many as 15 females on his stretch of beach.

Two bull pups, too young to fight for territory, play in the surf.

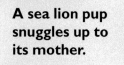

A sea lion pup snuggles up to its mother.

New Arrivals

Female sea lions give birth from June to August. They usually have one baby. But sometimes twins arrive. A few days after the pup is born, its mother **mates** again, with the bull who holds the territory. A new baby will then be born when the pup's mother returns to the beach the following year.

Baby mammals, such as mice and rabbits, are born in the safety of a snug nest or burrow. But baby sea lions are born on the open beach. Fortunately, they are usually surrounded by many other sea lions, which makes the beach safer for the pups. The adults can scare away any land predators that might try to attack a pup. The baby does not lie around helpless for long, within a few weeks it will be able to move quickly along the beach and swim in the sea.

Taking after Mother

A baby sea lion looks a lot like its mother, with big dark eyes, long whiskers, and slim flappy flippers. But, of course, it is tiny, and only weighs about 35 pounds (16 kg). Like all young mammals, the first food it wants is its mother's milk. Not long after birth it seeks out the milk and begins to drink.

The father plays no part in rearing the baby. He is usually too busy chasing other bulls—and any half-grown cows that try to join his harem—off his territory. Later the males leave the breeding beaches and head out to sea. They swim to distant fishing grounds where they spend fall and winter. The cows remain near the coast, where they can keep a close eye on their young.

A sea lion pup nestles against its mother.

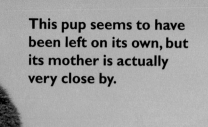

This pup seems to have been left on its own, but its mother is actually very close by.

Watchful Eye

Baby sea lions spend their time lying on the beach with many other pups. Most of the time their mother is there beside them. But sometimes she goes away to find food. However, when female seal lions leave their youngsters they keep a sharp lookout for danger. If the threat looks serious—for example, two bulls fighting over territory are about to roll over and crush her pup—she rushes back. She grabs her baby in her jaws and whisks it away to safety. Pups are not always aware of it, but female sea lions always keep a close eye on their youngsters.

Where's My Pup?

The mother seal remains with her baby full-time for its first week. After that she divides her time between **nursing** her baby and going on fishing trips. After a few days at sea she returns to the beach to face a whole herd of bleating pups!

To find her baby in the nursery of identical-looking youngsters, she calls for it. The pup answers with its own little bleat. As she reaches the youngster, she gives it a final sniff to confirm that it is hers, before allowing it to nurse.

The mother's milk gives the baby strength. The pup puts on weight rapidly. It begins to eat fish at about six months old. But it continues to drink its mother's milk through fall and winter, up until the time when she is ready to give birth again.

A sea lion pup answers
its mother's call.

A mother helps her
pup become confident
in the water.

Water Babies

The young sea lion gets its first swimming lesson at just ten days old. The mother begins the lesson by leading her pup into a calm, shallow tide pool. The youngster enjoys splashing about. If it feels tired, it scrambles onto its mother's back for a nap.

Because it only has a thin layer of blubber, at first the pup gets cold quite quickly. But as this fatty layer gets thicker, the pup spends more time in the water. After several weeks its mother leads it down to the vast ocean. It is soon ducking and diving among the crashing waves.

Playtime and After

By about four months old, the young sea lion is confident in the water. It spends hours playing with other pups—just messing about in the shallows or body-surfing in the breakers. There are long games of chase among the fronds of seaweed growing from the rocky bed.

By the age of six months, the youngster is fishing for itself. Winter turns to spring. When the mother goes ashore to have her next baby, the young sea lion hangs about by the edge of the rookery. Young cows do not start to have babies until they are six or seven years old, and young bulls do not breed until they are nine years old. But with luck the young sea lion will live to a ripe age of about 17, and have many pups of its own.

Words to Know

Aquatic   Relating to animals that live in water.

Blubber   The fatty layer next to a sea lion's skin, which keeps it warm in cold water.

Bulls   Male sea lions.

Cows   Female sea lions.

Gills   Feathery structures on a fish's head that allow the fish to breathe.

Harem   A group of female sea lions living with a male on a stretch of shore.

Mammals   Animals that have hair on their body and nourish their young on milk.

Mates   Comes together to produce young.

Molting   When an animal sheds its fur and grows a new coat.

Nursing	Drinking milk from the mother's body.
Peninsula	A thin piece of land stretching out to sea.
Pinnipeds	Members of the seal family.
Predators	Animals that hunt others for food.
Prey	An animal hunted by other animals.
Pup	A young sea lion.
Rookery	A stretch of beach or rocky shore where sea lions breed.
Species	The scientific word for animals of the same type that can breed together.
Territory	An area where an animal lives or breeds, and which it defends.
Webbed feet	Where the toes on an animal's feet are linked by skin, allowing them to act like paddles.

Find Out More

Books

Fetty, M. *Sea Lions*. New York: Bearport Publishing, 2007.

Shehata, K. and J. McElwee. *San Francisco's Famous Sea Lions*. Cincinnati, Ohio: Angel Bea Publishing, 2002.

Web sites

California Sea Lion
www.enchantedlearning.com/subjects/mammals/
pinniped/Sealionprintout.shtml
Facts about the California sea lion with a picture to print and color in.

Steller Sea Lions
www.sealioncaves.com/whatsee/steller.html
Information about northern sea lions and an audio file of them roaring.

Index